Immanent List Building

B. Vincent

Published by RWG Publishing, 2021.

IMMANENT LIST BUILDING

First edition. July 28, 2021.

Written by B. Vincent.

Also by B. Vincent

Bridge Pages
Business Acquisition
Business Bogging
Marketing Automation
Better Meetings
Conversion Optimization
Creative Solutions
Employee Recruitment
Startup Capital
Employee Mentoring
Servant Leadership
Human Resources
Team Building
Freelancing
Funnel Building
Geo Targeting
Goal Setting
Immanent List Building
Lead Generation

Table of Contents

Immanent List Building

Hi, and welcome to this seminar on impending rundown building. In this course, we'll tell you the best way to gather leads in the US naturally without your possibilities expecting to type anything into a structure. This course is separated into three modules. Module One gives you a short outline of this new idea. Module Two covers the apparatus we'll utilize and how to set it up, and module three goes over the novel subsequent missions you'll require. When this course is finished, you'll realize how to create leads naturally. In this way, right away, how about we plunge into the principal module.

Module One

Welcome to Module One. In this module, our master will give you a concise introduction to this new idea. Thus, prepare to take a few notes. Also, we should bounce directly in. Okay, so we should discuss this fascinating book. Also, to be honest, absolutely phenomenal type of rundown working, there is an extremely high probability that you have not known about this yet. It's new to the business somewhat new to the business. It is a type of lead age and rundown assembling that permits you to catch the email, the name and surprisingly the actual postage information of guests to your site, regardless of whether they didn't pick in or tap on anything in your site. What's more, the manner in which it does that depends on mysterious advanced identifiers of individuals who visit your site being coordinated against a goliath data set of genuine profiles of individuals in the United States. Presently, this is just in the United States that this should be possible. Or then again rather, the leads that you gather must be in the United States. In case you're outside the United States, and you need to participate in this present, it's clearly vital that you address your business legal advisors, your lawyers. Furthermore, truth be told, that is continually something to do in any case, even in the United States. In any case, in the United States, we do have commonly notable can spam laws. OK, and this is 100% agreeable with those. It's in consistence with the can spam guidelines. It's in consistence with ccpa. What's more, with the entirety of the material guidelines and decides and laws that you can discover in the United States. Along these lines, it's incredibly, painstakingly created in a way that is absolutely legitimately genuine. Regardless of whether it sounds somewhat unrealistic. Presently, what this catches isn't each guest, truth be told, by and large, it will be a minority.

Yet, as per this device, they can very match a 70% of the guests that go to your site to something like one identifier in their information base. The apparatus is called get messages. Also, it works by putting a pixel on your site that gets it sees it dissects, and it gets those unknown computerized identifiers. Also, it looks at those identifiers of your guests to their data set. Also, in case there's a match, it adds those individuals their names, their messages, and your the actual street number to your rundown to your rundown of leads. Also, in case you're pondering, how would they do that lawfully? Like I said, it's all agreeable with ccpa. What's more, can spam act and every one of the principles and guidelines. Looking at the situation objectively today, a many individuals, a many individuals have selected in and click the Yes button on, you know, arrangements for things like Facebook or 1000 different sites that they use, in which they are permitted to. Furthermore, by they I mean the destinations that they're concurring that they're consenting to these arrangements with, they're permitted to bring those identifiers into a data set. Alright. What's more, the information base is extremely enormous in the United States. It's extremely, huge. The data set being referred to here, is related with around 250 million people in the US as per this instrument. So we need to recognize here that there is a reason for a conversation of morals. Here. Numerous individuals feel that something isn't really moral, just in light of the fact that it's lawful. What's more, that is valid. This, notwithstanding, would appear to be one could put forth the defense one could contend that it just ascents to the degree of possibly irritating individuals. That since everything's done effectively, as per the material laws and guidelines. Also, everything depends on assent that individuals gave sooner or later, et cetera. that there isn't actually any huge worry with morals.

There is a worry However, with inconvenience, irritation, thus you must be extremely cautious with this in case you will utilize this instrument, and that is truly going to come up in the subsequent meet-ups. You will send these individuals after they've joined your rundown dependent on those unknown computerized identifiers. What's more, that will be canvassed in the last module number three. In any case, this device is exceptionally viable. Furthermore, it has extremely top notch data, exceptionally excellent leads that you're getting. They have exceptionally cautious calculations, in which they just pass on individuals who have been dynamic inside their organization in their information base inside the most recent 14 days. What's more, they likewise scour it for individuals who have been known to grumble and withdraw a ton. Isn't that so? So you're truly getting exceptionally excellent leads onto your rundown here. Furthermore, they've demonstrated that you can get some excellent and positive select in rates, and some shockingly low protest rates. OK, there will be objections, there's no doubt. It's an exceptionally clever idea and an original technique. Furthermore, individuals are getting messages from you that they truly didn't agree to, essentially not in the customary sense.

As there will be objections, however they're shockingly low, shockingly low. What's more, truth be told, this instrument guarantees that the objection rates are not as much as point 1%. Alright, which is, once more, shockingly low, they work effectively of scouring and cleaning, similar to I referenced. Also, they do, truth be told, regard buyer security, in light of the fact that each individual who is in this data set has picked in to the organization or the information base previously. Furthermore, they really keep up with records of the date in which they selected in, and the URL for it and all that great stuff. Presently, a many individuals say, Well, you know, when individuals pick in, at times this is on the grounds that they had a bit, you know, a lawful spring up on their page that said, I acknowledge and they were sluggish, and they clicked, I acknowledge. Furthermore, sure there's discussion about that. Furthermore, individuals are allowed to concur or differ about the subtleties and its morals, et cetera. In any case, the truth of the matter is, it is totally lawfully consistent. What's more, it is an alternative that you're surely ready to consider in case you're working together in the United States.

Eventually, the advantage of doing this is that you're getting more messages, you're getting an approach to contact individuals who have communicated some interest in your business since they went to your site. What's more, by far most of individuals who go to your site or to your, your web properties, your presentation pages, wind up leaving, and they're gone perpetually, and you can't get in touch with them. Indeed, presently a critical level of them can be reached. What's more, I get messages has shown that that can really convert into recovering 20% of your income at times. So even for the situation, where you're just getting a minority of guests who go to your site, who can be coordinated against this data set and added to your email show, it's an inconceivable advantage, on the grounds that those are individuals who you would now be able to connect with in a proper manner, we'll talk about that in Module Three. Be that as it may, those are individuals who you would now be able to contact who you in any case would not have had the option to connect with. Also, that means only uplifting news for your business. Thus this is an exceptionally cool device. Once more, there's a lot of space for discussion and conflict in regards to the topic of morals, and, you know, irritation, etc. Furthermore, nobody needs to utilize this apparatus, yet it's a significant one to realize that is out there. Furthermore, I think the potential advantages simply all by themselves, aside from all the other things are quite clear. Furthermore, that this is an apparatus unquestionably worth investigating. Thus in the following module, we're really going to go into the actual instrument, we will see how to set it up what's in store inside how to glue the pixel on your site and how it all kind of practically functions. And afterward in the module from that point forward, we'll take a gander at the rationale and the style of follow up that you should utilize. Since once more, this is extremely extraordinary. So how about we feel free to continue on to the following module.

Module Two

Welcome to Module Two. In this module, our master will cover the uncommon device we'll utilize. So prepare to take a few notes. Furthermore, how about we hop directly in. Okay, so here we are within the get messages account. This is the dashboard. All we will do in this module is click around and kind of, you know, take a gander at how things work in here. Also, you realize how to explore the site and at last get your pixel code and utilize the item by putting your pixel on your page. So this is the dashboard, similar to I said, you can really see the graph that demonstrates you know, your contacts that were gained throughout a given timeframe. This here is really a lunch period that we had in November. So we had an item dispatch where we had an entire pack of deals coming in, we had a ton of individuals going to our site. Also, indeed, as is typically the case by far most of them left without taking any kind of action, then, at that point it's continually going to be the situation on a business page or a select in page. A great many people will leave without taking any kind of action. For this situation, we really got a sum of 728 of those contacts what we in any case would not have gotten they didn't select into an email rundown and they didn't accepting anything. Yet, we do can contact them and send some sort of correspondence to them, since it was snatched here.

Presently there is and they're displaying it here there is a capacity with get messages to follow your incomes. Furthermore, that is by setting certain codes, a more particular codes on the pages of your site showing what they address as far as, you know, a deal, you know, so the achievement page in the wake of buying, you know, a specific item may be valued at $30, right, thus get messages realizes that after it arrives on that page, or for this situation, it really coordinates with Shopify, so it's likely substantially more smoothed out than that. Yet, you know, essentially, you can sort out dependent on individuals showing up on specific pages, and their association with your site, how much cash was made. What's more, that is, that is really cool that you can follow that within getting messages. Yet, at the present time, in this record, we're simply utilizing it to gather the prompts gather the names, the messages, and the postage information. As should be obvious, here, an entire pack of contacts gathered, you can see that around the hour of that dispatch in November, we had a gigantic flood of contacts coming in. What's more, those are generally individuals who we would now be able to email market to, and they're totally gathered here in the downloadable contacts area. Furthermore, what you used to need to do, contingent upon which plan you're on, was physically gather these individuals after a specific timeframe.

Presently, everything's constant. Furthermore, you can really come here to the reconciliations tab. What's more, you can really incorporate with your email showcasing programming or your outsider applications for sure have you, to naturally have the contact data shipped off your different advertising stages surprisingly, progressively. So extremely, cool that you can do that at this point. So you have the dashboard mixes contact, the following thing you have is the code piece, the code scrap. Presently for the code piece, this is really significant. This is the main part of this really, this is the place where you will get the piece of code that you need to append to your site, what you will do is you will come here to the your content spring up, that surfaces. Also, as should be obvious, there's no code in there yet, in light of the fact that you haven't determined what kind of code it is. What you need to decide for gathering is clearly assortment, not concealment, alright. concealment implies don't give me contacts who have been on this page, whatever page, you wind up putting this bit on.

Alright, income following, similar to I said, is the further developed thing where you're going to kind of get an impression of how much cash you made dependent on individuals arriving on specific pages, etc. So cool element, we're not going to get into that at this moment. We're taking a gander at the center part of get messages, and that is gathering messages of guests. So we will go with assortment, what you would do is you would get this code, you'd duplicate it, and afterward you would head toward your site page. What's more, you know, contingent upon which content administration framework you're utilizing, in case you're utilizing WordPress, or clickfunnels, or Instapage, it will be unique. In any case, it's really going to be practically the same, the entire idea, and you've presumably done this previously, you've most likely stuck contents, similar to Google Tag Manager, or your Facebook following pixel, et cetera. In any case, fundamentally, you've approached any place you do that in your foundation, and you place it into the proper following contents area, it doesn't really determine here, what segment to place it in. So I'm expecting it doesn't make any difference to an extreme. Definitely, the lone the lone distinction here is the request wherein things get stacked on your page. Furthermore, this case, that doesn't really matter excessively, I don't think thus you can place it in the header segment or in the body or in the footer area, you would glue that here. What's more, you need to ensure that it's difficult by and large on your site, we hypothetically you could do that assuming you need it to. Yet, what you truly need to do is center around which page you're following, so you can, in your subsequent meet-ups make references to what the individual was taking a gander at. Right, and we'll discuss the significance of the exceptionally special style of subsequent meet-ups that you will send in the following module. Yet, that that makes it even more essential to attempt to utilize particularity with which pages you're connecting your content to. And afterward, you know, use particularity once more, with the messages that you're sending, in view of which pages they visited, and how you gathered them.

So for instance, suppose you have a site and one piece of your site you're selling, you know, drills and another piece of your site, you're selling paste, correct? It's most likely a smart thought to set up an alternate bit for every one of those so that in your email, you can specify the way that they looked at your site and we're keen on your paste. And afterward you can have a connection in there that they can tap on, which will permit you to you know, measure their conduct and their cooperation etc, which we'll get into that in Module Three in any case. In any case, explicitness is acceptable. As I'm saying explicitness is acceptable. So having an alternate ones For the various kinds of things that they may be cooperating with on your site page is a smart thought. Yet, that is the manner by which you do that here. It's quite straightforward, exceptionally basic. Basically the same as snatching you know your fixed Facebook retargeting pixel or your Google remarketing labels, et cetera. So that is the code pieces, concealment records. That is fundamentally where you reveal to them that somebody who's on this page is somebody who you would prefer not to gather. Furthermore, the most clear illustration of this would be essentially individuals who get to your thank you page subsequent to picking into your rundown, right. Also, let me clarify the rationale here. So suppose you have a greeting page, a lead age page where individuals can type in their email address, right. And afterward you have the thank you page, or perhaps it's a tripwire, or an upsell page from that point forward, whatever it is the page that they get to just in the event that they composed in their email address on the main page, correct? In the event that they get to that subsequent page, that implies that they as of now deliberately gave you their email address.

So you would prefer not to get messages to snatch their email, in this other novel technique, isn't that so? This novel way to deal with getting their messages, it's, it's excess, and it can possibly cause issues. Thus on the off chance that they arrived on that page, it implies that you have their email address in the customary manner. So you don't have to gather it along these lines. Alright, or possibly you would like to, you may have your own reasons. Yet, the overall winning rationale would be that, you know, in case you're as of now gathering them, you just get a specific number of contacts each month that you're paying for. You would prefer not to squander that on individuals whose email tends to you previously got, on the grounds that they picked in, you just need individuals who didn't select in. Right. Thus concealment list is a way that you would do that. How about we see your patterns, simply an approach to break down and track your information, occasion detail. That is for empower income following to follow deals and ROI access that has to do with the, you know, the real more top to bottom and complex following, to see the viability of your traffic and the income that you're creating, we discussed that as of now. And afterward support, I know, there's a toss out the manual attitude among numerous individuals in the web showcasing space. In any case, for this situation, since it truly is, it quite is a novel and one of a kind and new idea, which isn't something that happens frequently in the space. This is a region where you really would like to invest some energy you would like to peruse this, you would like to ensure that you have a decent comprehension of how to get things done. Also, you know, the why and the then the need and, you know, ensure you're understanding this apparatus, since it is new, and it's remarkable. And afterward that makes it even more significant. However, that is fundamentally a walkthrough of the get messages account region, and how to set it up on your greeting page. The main piece of the entirety of this is the manner by which to circle back to these individuals since it must be done in an extremely cautious and novel manner, it isn't possible in the customary advertising way, since they didn't deliberately all things considered. Keep in mind, legitimately talking, they did, on the grounds that they agreed to something before. In any case, they didn't deliberately and explicitly select in to your rundown such that they comprehend or recollect. Thus you truly must be cautious and purposeful. What's more, handle is in a novel way when you're sending your first email to them. Furthermore, we'll talk about that in the following module.

Module Three

Welcome to Module Three. In this module, our master will cover the one of a kind subsequent missions you'll require. So prepare to take a few notes and how about we hop directly in. Okay, so this is potentially the main piece of this preparation, the subsequent missions, these will be incredibly, extraordinary and altogether different they must be they must be okay, and the reasons are self-evident, in light of the fact that these individuals didn't select in to your rundown. Furthermore, in this way you can't market to them. Similarly that you market to your standard endorser rundown or client rundown of individuals who have selected in or buy things from you, you just can't. You will have strange degrees of spam and grievances and withdraws and things that are simply going to obliterate your deliverability. Right, which is the reason you ought to really be utilizing a different autoresponder for this kind of rundown. Your unknown lead age rundown ought to be in an alternate autoresponder and an alternate email area so it doesn't affect your customary email advertising.

Right. So you need a few mechanizations set up that individuals get through that are exceptionally interesting and we'll discuss that in a second. Right, however you need individuals to get through those mechanizations by means of an email from area directly from address with a from email space that is unique in relation to your normal email advertising right and ideally an autoresponder account or an alternate autoresponder programming by and large. That is not quite the same as your normal email advertising. You need them to go through this succession of advertising, exceptionally novel showcasing first. And afterward whenever they've finished the robotization or the excursion such that you're happy with, then, at that point you can redesign them to and move them on to your primary rundown dependent on their conduct, right. So in the event that they've opened your messages and clicked your connections, and interfaced, etc, you know, you can set up triggers that cause them to then be added with an API mix, for instance, suppose, or in any event, something outsider like Zapier, that can make them be added to your customary email advertising. In any case, you must utilize this as a channel, and it must be detached with the goal that it doesn't cut down the entirety of your customary email advertising. So for what reason does this need to be so unique? For what reason is it such nothing to joke about that your subsequent missions are so not the same as your normal email promoting, follow up crusades, this is on the grounds that they didn't select in. Also, countless them will be irate, or irritated or befuddled. Isn't that so? That it's a horrible idea to clearly, you can't say something clear, as, Hey, much obliged for joining my rundown, or a debt of gratitude is in order for mentioning such and such, on the grounds that they didn't compose, you can't say something to that effect. Yet additionally the tone, it's difficult the words, however the tone of the email should be altogether different. Alright, you need to say something in your first email to them.

Compose your first spontaneous, you had the opportunity to remember that, your first spontaneous email to them, you need to say something that sounds favorable, and regular and coherent enough to fit the circumstance. Also, I'll be straightforward, the least demanding approach to do that is an exceptionally short email that recognizes that they visited your site. Alright, that is really the most straightforward approach to do this present, it's the way that will presumably get you minimal measure of contact, right. So suppose somebody goes to your site, suppose you sell, I don't have the foggiest idea, suppose you sell gas generators, right reinforcement generators, and somebody went to your site, and afterward they left, and you have their email now, due to this unique programming. Correct? What you would send is something extremely straightforward. something as per in light of the fact that you're gathering their name here, as well, you could say, Bob, simply needed to express profound gratitude for looking at our site today. In the event that you need more data on XYZ generators, we have an extraordinary article here, you know, then, at that point you have a connection that they can tap on, right, you need something that they can tap on to communicate with, in light of the fact that you need triggers, you need to have the option to channel dependent on their conduct that is truly significant. You know, you need them to have a chance to communicate, in light of the fact that once they associate, that demonstrates that they are keen on your substance, right. What's more, you can utilize that as one of your triggers or your channels for who endures this entire cycle and onto your ordinary email list, your customary email promoting measure. So you need to ensure that you referenced the way that they visited your site, you're still be encouraged, you're actually going to get some contact, you're actually going to get individuals saying, Wait a moment, I didn't pick in, they will recollect, much of the time, they will recall that they went to your site, and they didn't select in. What's more, they may send you an awful fabulous, they may blow up, they may withdraw, they may hit the spam button. Be that as it may, in the event that you keep it kind, you keep it truly benevolent.

Hello, much obliged for looking at our site today. Inform me as to whether you have any inquiries, click here to book a call, we have an incredible article here or parting with a free, you know, XYZ, simply click here to get it. Right and make that as frictionless as could really be expected, on the grounds that you needn't bother with them to select in on the grounds that you as of now have their email address. So you know, simply make them something that they can in a real sense simply snatch possibly a connection, you realize something to acquire a tad of generosity, keep it favorable and straightforward and wonderful. Also, that will be the awesome, approach to do this. What's more, I would prefer not to frighten you to an extreme, you're not likely going to have a gigantic, tremendous measure of individuals grumbling, the vast majority will presumably disregard the messages, that is the thing that a great many people will in general do. Be that as it may, clearly, you will have an altogether higher pace of spam or grievances than you ordinarily would on a customary email list. Clearly, it simply bodes well. Yet, numerous individuals are simply going to disregard them. Numerous individuals will open them and they may give you know, five seconds of thought to the way that Wait a moment, I didn't pick in to anything, I didn't buy in. And afterward quickly, you know, disregard that and continue on and click on the connection that you sent them. What's more, I'll be straightforward, a many individuals and we're living in the time of email advertising and select ins and buying in and stuff. A many individuals aren't in any event, going to see it. A many individuals will not recollect that they didn't select in they'll accept that they should expect that they probably picked in you know, and different clarifications may exist. Goodness definitely, that that site most likely had one of those, you know, login with Facebook catches or, or something like that. You know, there's so numerous ways that individuals are accustomed to picking into things, you know, coincidentally or not really accidentally, however in a way that was not straightforwardly identified with the activity that they needed to do.

Those, you know, login with Facebook API combinations are an ideal illustration of that. The rate at which individuals are utilized to simply composing in their email address, or really, the autofill highlight on the vast majority's workstations and work areas and cell phones, you know, where they simply happen a field and blast, their email address springs up as a choice, and they tap that and they can, they can regularly so rapidly, individuals are so used to doing that, in a particularly lighthearted and, and practically careless way. that as a rule, they will not understand that they didn't pick in to your rundown, they will not be aware of it, they'll simply accept that they did. Thus the adverse outcomes won't be horrible. I'm making an effort not to panic you with the entire thought that you know, you're going to, you will get cooked by these individuals. In any case, I do that the explanation I'm focusing on the expanded rate that you will see of grumblings and spam and you know, awful grams is basically to make it understood and commute home the point that you truly need to keep this detached from your ordinary email showcasing, don't, I rehash, don't coordinate this straightforwardly to your standard email advertising programming. Thus the following inquiry is, how would you proceed with the discussion? How would you proceed with the discussion after the underlying development? All things considered, I would say the a few messages that you send in a robotization grouping should all be similar a few messages ought to be equivalent to that initial one, extremely generous, you know, very, kind of casually recognizing that they visited your site, and afterward giving them something, a connection to a blog entry or something that they can tap on, so you see their communication with your messages, or see whether they collaborated by any means. And afterward you can kind of slide into some more customary showcasing from here on out. Alright, on the grounds that a many individuals, regardless of whether they didn't open your messages, or regardless of whether they, you know, taken a gander at your messages and blew up, or irritated or confounded, after they've seen them a few times skimming around with the other, you know, 500 advertising messages that they get each day, it's simply going to kind of normally resolve itself, you know, and you will be a name that they're accustomed to finding in their inbox. Also, on the off chance that they don't care for it, they'll withdraw, correct? So you can progressively after a few extremely delicate and casual, and, and considerate, early on messages, similar to the ones we referenced, bit by bit slip them into some more conventional showcasing. And afterward I would say, in light of their conduct, all through your computerization grouping, in view of whether they opened and regardless of whether they clicked etc, then, at that point set up certain robotizations and a few triggers, that will make them be moved over to your customary rundown to your principle list. That sort of bodes well.

Presently, another subsequent inquiry here, on the grounds that with this product, you are, as we referenced, ready to get the actual street number, the postal location, and that is tremendous, in light of the fact that postal addresses or pardon me, postage, you know, advertising, promoting through actual mail is an entire distinctive ballgame. You know, it's more separated, it will just by its tendency, since it's actual mail, it'll be, you know, days after they visited your site, you know, so they're bound to not recollect that, they're bound to not, you know, have a negative understanding of accepting your message via the post office. Thus you don't need to be as cautious you don't need to, you know, behave like you're strolling around on eggshells with the actual mail, you know, assuming you need to, you can send them a letter or postcard that recognizes that they visited your site assuming you need to, however I don't feel like the need is as fundamental there. In light of the way that individuals consider and handle, you know, actual mail, which they most likely arrange as garbage mail when it's special. What's more, on the grounds that the blowback isn't as terrible you know, there's no spam button that they can tap on their actual letter box that will adversely affect your email promoting, you know, or get your record closed down or get you know, your from address, you know, the email, space of your from address, to lose cool focuses with the ESP is et cetera. Right. Along these lines, actual mail, you don't need to truly be treading lightly, yet at the same time put some idea into it and ensure that you know, you're advertising to them legitimately fits the situation that they're in, you know, the way that you've secretly snatched their actual postage information, lawfully, however namelessly. In view of a site visit, simply remember that when you're planning the offer, that you're sending them via the post office and the phrasing that you're utilizing etc. Yet, the truly significant thing is keeping your email advertising disconnected, and ensure that those initial not many subsequent meet-ups are written in a kind, casual way, altogether different from your conventional promoting and afterward step by step slip them into your customary showcasing. Furthermore, ensure you consider their conduct and their cooperations when you're deciding when and if to move them from that disengaged circumstance into your standard email showcasing, programming and computerizations.

Don't miss out!

Visit the website below and you can sign up to receive emails whenever B. Vincent publishes a new book. There's no charge and no obligation.

https://books2read.com/r/B-A-QWUO-PTUQB

BOOKS 2 READ

Connecting independent readers to independent writers.

Also by B. Vincent

Affiliate Marketing
Affiliate Marketing
Affiliate Marketing

Standalone
Affiliate Recruiting
Business Layoffs & Firings
Business and Entrepreneur Guide
Business Remote Workforce
Career Transition
Project Management
Precision Targeting
Professional Development
Strategic Planning
Content Marketing
Imminent List Building
Getting Past GateKeepers
Banner Ads
Bookkeeping

Bridge Pages
Business Acquisition
Business Bogging
Marketing Automation
Better Meetings
Conversion Optimization
Creative Solutions
Employee Recruitment
Startup Capital
Employee Mentoring
Servant Leadership
Human Resources
Team Building
Freelancing
Funnel Building
Geo Targeting
Goal Setting
Immanent List Building
Lead Generation

About the Publisher

Accepting manuscripts in the most categories. We love to help people get their words available to the world.

Revival Waves of Glory focus is to provide more options to be published. We do traditional paperbacks, hardcovers, audio books and ebooks all over the world. A traditional royalty-based publisher that offers self-publishing options, Revival Waves provides a very author friendly and transparent publishing process, with President Bill Vincent involved in the full process of your book. Send us your manuscript and we will contact you as soon as possible.

Contact: Bill Vincent at rwgpublishing@yahoo.com www.rwgpublishing.com

www.ingramcontent.com/pod-product-compliance
Lightning Source LLC
Chambersburg PA
CBHW030535210326
41597CB00014B/1164